OLYMPIC SPORTS

OLYMPIC GYMNASTICS

BY CHRÖS McDOUGALL

SportsZone

An Imprint of Abdo Publishing
abdobooks.com

abdobooks.com

Published by Abdo Publishing, a division of ABDO, PO Box 398166, Minneapolis, Minnesota 55439.

Printed in the United States of America, North Mankato, Minnesota.
102024
012025

THIS BOOK CONTAINS
RECYCLED MATERIALS

Cover Photo: Ezra Shaw/Getty Images Sport/Getty Images
Interior Photos: Sean Garnsworthy/Getty Images Sport/Getty Images, 5; Kristian Dowling/Getty Images Sport/Getty Images, 7; Alex Livesey/Getty Images Sport/Getty Images, 8; Maja Hitij/Getty Images Sport/Getty Images, 10; Tom Weller/VOIGT/Getty Images Sport/Getty Images, 13; Sepia Times/Universal Images Group/Getty Images, 15; Scherl/Sueddeutsche Zeitung Photo/Alamy, 16; Heinz Wieseler/picture alliance/Getty Images, 19; Julian Finney/Getty Images Sport/Getty Images, 22; Lionel Bonaventure/AFP/Getty Images, 23; Keystone-France/Gamma-Keystone/Getty Images, 25; ullstein bild Dtl./Getty Images, 27; Keystone/Hulton Archive/Getty Images, 29; Wally McNamee/Corbis Historical/Getty Images, 32; Focus On Sport/Getty Images Sport/Getty Images, 33; David Madison/Getty Images Sport/Getty Images, 35, 36; Chris McGrath/Getty Images Sport/Getty Images, 39; Tim Clayton/Corbis Sport/Getty Images, 41; Ronald Martinez/Getty Images Sport/Getty Images, 42; Wei Zheng/ChinaSports/Visual China Group/Getty Images, 45

Editor: Haley Williams
Series Designer: Karli Kruse

Library of Congress Control Number: 2024938358

Publisher's Cataloging-in-Publication Data

Names: McDougall, Chrös, author.
Title: Olympic gymnastics / by Chrös McDougall
Description: Minneapolis, Minnesota: ABDO Publishing, 2025 | Series: Olympic sports | Includes online resources and index.
Identifiers: ISBN 9781098295493 (lib. bdg.) | ISBN 9798384916499 (ebook)
Subjects: LCSH: Olympic games--Juvenile literature. | Gymnastics--Juvenile literature. | Olympians (Olympic athletes)--Juvenile literature. | Olympics--History--Juvenile literature. | Sports--Juvenile literature.
Classification: DDC 796.44--dc23

TABLE OF CONTENTS

CHAPTER 1

AMERICAN DYNASTY

Carly Patterson stepped onto the floor, bowed her head, and took a breath. One routine remained in the women's gymnastics all-around final at the 2004 Olympic Games in Athens, Greece. The gold medal was in reach. And when the music kicked in, Patterson went for it.

The 16-year-old from Allen, Texas, leaped and danced her way to one corner of the floor. Then she charged across the floor for a tumbling pass, finishing it with a full-twisting double back tuck. As the routine went on, Patterson only seemed to gain confidence. She moved with precision. She appeared to float through the air on her jumps. And when she landed back on the floor, she did so with complete control.

It had not been a perfect night for Patterson. She had stepped out of bounds on vault during the first rotation. That put her in eighth place. But she moved to fourth place after a strong showing on the uneven bars. Then a stunning and

Carly Patterson helped the United States win silver in the women's team final at the 2004 Olympics.

difficult performance on balance beam pushed her into first. She just needed a strong score on floor to hold off Russia's Svetlana Khorkina, the reigning world champion.

Patterson powered through one more high-flying tumbling pass. Then she smiled, knowing she had just completed an all-time performance. Soon after, the judges confirmed it. With a score of 9.712, Patterson defeated Khorkina by .176. That made Patterson only the second US woman to win the all-around gold medal, and the first to win it in 20 years. Little did Patterson know at the time, but her win set off what would become a new era of dominance by American women in Olympic gymnastics.

AN AMERICAN ERA

Women have been competing in artistic gymnastics at the Olympics since 1928. The individual all-around gold medal was first awarded in 1952. But it wasn't until 32 years later that an American first medaled in the event. West Virginia's Mary Lou Retton broke through with her thrilling performance for gold at the 1984 Games in Los Angeles. Then Shannon Miller of Oklahoma won all-around silver at the 1992 Olympics in Barcelona, Spain.

Patterson's 2004 performance put Team USA atop the podium once again. Four years later, US teammates

Shawn Johnson and Nastia Liukin arrived at the 2008 Games in Beijing, China, as the clear all-around favorites. In a captivating final, the balletic Liukin held off her more energetic and powerful teammate Johnson. Liukin won gold, and Johnson claimed silver. Then at the 2012 Olympics in London, England, Gabby Douglas capped off a rapid rise through elite gymnastics with an all-around gold medal of her own.

Nastia Liukin, *right*, and Shawn Johnson finished the 2008 Games with a combined nine medals.

Simone Biles flips above the beam during the women's all-around final at the 2016 Olympics.

THE NEXT LEVEL

Simone Biles arrived in Rio de Janeiro, Brazil, for the 2016 Olympics as the clear favorite to win the all-around. She had already won the all-around title at the previous three World Championships. In Rio, the 19-year-old Texan showed why people were already calling her the greatest of all time.

Some gymnasts thrive on their exquisite technique. Others rack up points by performing the most difficult skills. Biles excelled in both areas. Packing tremendous power into her 4-foot-8 frame, Biles made the most difficult skills look easy. At the 2016 Games, she set the tone in the first rotation with a huge vault. Then she nailed her routine on the uneven bars, which many people consider her weakest event. Some were surprised to see the standings still close at the midway point. But the reigning balance beam and floor exercise world champion took over in the last two rotations.

Biles barely flinched while tumbling and spinning around the narrow balance beam. Then in an explosive floor routine, she unleashed her massive tumbling as the crowd cheered on every move. Upon striking her final pose, Biles knew she had done it. The US coach at that time said the routine was very close to perfection.

The United States became the first country to win four consecutive individual all-around gold medals. And when Biles announced she was coming back for the 2020 Olympics in Tokyo, Japan, most people expected that winning streak to extend to five. But no one could have predicted how it unfolded.

A global pandemic postponed the Games to 2021. Fans were not allowed into the stadiums. Many athletes felt anxious and isolated. And in the women's team final, Biles experienced "the twisties." That meant her mind and body were not clicking while she tumbled. At risk of serious injury, Biles withdrew from the team final, and then the all-around as well. But in her place, teammate Suni Lee stepped into the spotlight.

Suni Lee was named the 2021 Female Athlete of the Year by *Sports Illustrated* magazine after her performance in Tokyo.

The 18-year-old Minnesotan opened with perhaps her best vault ever. Then came the uneven bars. When on top of her game, Lee could perform an impossibly difficult routine. And in the all-around final, she did just that. Connecting an exhausting and complex series of swings and releases, Lee earned a score of 15.300, tying for the best of the night on the event. Then she strung together two more strong showings on balance beam and floor exercise. When the final scores showed, Lee had done just enough to hold off the vibrant Brazilian Rebeca Andrade for gold. Lee's win kept Team USA's gold medal streak alive.

MAKE IT SIX

Biles did not know if she would ever compete again after Tokyo. Lee wanted to, but two kidney diseases left her sick throughout 2023. Yet when the 2024 Olympics kicked off in Paris, France, both Americans were there.

Biles once again arrived as the favorite. She had returned to competition the previous summer

HISTORIC FIRSTS

In addition to racking up Olympic medals, several US women have broken ground in other ways at the Games. Dominique Dawes competed in three Olympics. At her second in Atlanta in 1996, she became the first Black gymnast to win an individual medal. Gabby Douglas's all-around gold in 2012 was the first for a Black gymnast. Simone Biles made it two in a row in 2016. Then, in 2021, Suni Lee became the first Asian American gymnast to win the all-around title.

and added to her international medal haul. With seven Olympic medals, plus 30 from the World Championships, Biles was the sport's most decorated athlete. Meanwhile, Lee had gotten her medical setbacks under control. She appeared to be getting better with each performance. But extending the US all-around winning streak was no guarantee.

Never was that clearer for Biles than after the second rotation in Paris. She struggled through her uneven bars routine. At one point, her feet nearly touched the mat. Suddenly, Biles found herself sitting in third place, and Lee was back in fifth. Catching first-place Andrade would be no easy task.

Balance beam was next. Biles confidently mounted the apparatus. Her abilities on beam were well established. And with the world watching, she cruised through her difficult routine. The rock-solid performance earned Biles the top beam score of the night. It also shot her back into first place. Lee, meanwhile, followed with a strong performance of her own on beam. Then she closed the night with another big score on the floor exercise.

Only Andrade and Biles remained. Once again, the Brazilian shined in her floor routine. But Biles opened floor with the most difficult tumbling pass ever performed in women's gymnastics, the triple twisting double back. By the time she

At the 2024 Games, Simone Biles and Suni Lee became the first former Olympic all-around champions to compete against each other in the women's all-around final.

saluted the judges to end her routine, everyone knew who had won. Biles became just the third woman to win a pair of all-around gold medals. Lee joined her on the podium in third. It marked the first time two former all-around champions stood on the podium together. And, for the seventh time, an American woman was the Olympic all-around champion.

CHAPTER 2

ANCIENT ORIGINS, MODERN SPORT

A new movement was beginning in the late 1800s. French educator Pierre de Coubertin had been inspired by the ancient Greek Olympics. He wanted to recreate the event on a global stage. And in April 1896, his vision came to life. More than 240 athletes from 14 countries arrived in Athens to take part in the first modern Olympic Games.

Artistic gymnastics was among 10 sports contested in Athens. Like the Olympics themselves, gymnastics had ancient origins. However, ancient gymnastics barely resembled the modern sport. The term *gymnastics* referred to a variety of exercises and physical challenges held in a gymnasium. Young men took part in gymnastics to prepare for war. During the 1800s, gymnastics began developing into the sport it is today. Even so, early Olympic gymnastics would look almost unrecognizable to today's fans.

Before the first modern Olympics, athletes took part in gymnastics festivals to show off their skills. The first festival was held in Germany in 1860.

Parallel bars and high bar were the only gymnastics team events at the 1896 Olympics.

In 1896, people from different countries had varying ideas about what gymnastics competitions should look like. Some gymnastics competitions even included swimming or track-and-field events. For the Olympics, officials embraced a German form of the sport in which athletes performed using fixed apparatuses. Some apparatuses have been around from the start. Gymnasts at the 1896 Games performed routines on the high bar, parallel bars, pommel horse, still rings, and vault. Those apparatuses, along with floor exercise, still make up men's gymnastics today. But other early events, such as rope climbing, club swinging, and side horse, did not stick.

Other early trends did not last either. For example, gymnastics competitions used to take place outdoors. But perhaps the biggest difference from that era was that only men were allowed to take part in early Olympic gymnastics.

Coubertin, like many people at the time, believed sports were too exhausting for women. As a result, all the athletes at the 1896 Olympics were men. Only a handful of women took part in the Games that followed in 1900. After Coubertin left his role leading the International Olympic Committee in 1925, women gained more opportunities. Nearly twice as many women competed at the 1928 Games than in 1924. The 1928 Olympics in Amsterdam, Netherlands, were also the first to include women's gymnastics.

Gymnastics officials designed the women's program to "align with traditional female values," such as flexibility and grace. Women also competed on different apparatuses than the men. These differences made the sport more acceptable to Olympic officials. Nearly a century later, distinct differences remain between men's and women's gymnastics. Women compete on four apparatuses, which are floor exercise, vault, balance beam, and uneven bars. Men, on the other hand, have six apparatuses, giving them two extra medal opportunities. Since 1960, men and women each have a team and individual all-around event, plus individual finals on each apparatus.

GYMNASTICS POWERS

Many elements of modern gymnastics were developed in Germany. So it was little surprise when German gymnasts won five of the eight events at the 1896 Olympics. Western European countries continued to thrive at the Olympics into the 1930s. Among the strongest countries was Italy. It won four of the five men's team gold medals between 1912 and 1932.

World War II (1939–45) forced a 12-year break for the Olympics. Soon after the Games resumed in 1948, the Soviet Union took over Olympic gymnastics. From 1952 to 1980, the Soviet women won every team gold medal. And the Soviet men won three team gold medals. Also during that period, Japan's

The United States, along with more than 60 other countries, boycotted the 1980 Olympics in Moscow, Soviet Union.

men's team began establishing a dynasty of its own by winning five gold medals. Meanwhile, the small Eastern European country of Romania emerged as a women's power in the 1970s. In 1980, China returned to the Olympics following a 28-year absence. It quickly joined the gymnastics elite as well.

One country that did not have a great gymnastics tradition at that time was the United States. The sport finally surged in popularity during the 1970s. Then, in 1984, the Olympics were held in Los Angeles. Four years earlier, the United States led a boycott of the 1980 Games in Moscow, Soviet Union.

RHYTHMIC GYMNASTICS

In 1984, a second gymnastics discipline was added to the Olympics. Rhythmic gymnastics is a women's-only sport. The athletes perform routines to music while using one of four handheld apparatuses. These are the ribbon, hoop, ball, and clubs. There is also a rhythmic group event in which five gymnasts perform together. Russia and other Eastern European countries have thrived in Olympic rhythmic gymnastics. Russia's Evgenia Kanaeva became the first rhythmic gymnast to win consecutive individual gold medals, doing so in 2008 and 2012.

In response, the Soviets boycotted the 1984 Games. This opened the door for a breakthrough performance that helped boost the United States into one of the world's top contenders.

In 1991, the Soviet Union broke into 15 independent countries. Former Soviet athletes competed as the Unified Team in 1992, winning both the men's and women's team gold medals. Gymnasts from former Soviet republics, including Russia, Ukraine, and Belarus, continued to thrive in the years to come.

However, a few countries have stood above the rest. From 1992 to 2024, China, Japan, and versions of the Russian team won 20 of the 27 available Olympic men's team medals. Meanwhile, the US women's team medaled in every Olympics during that same time. That included gold medals in 1996, 2012, 2016, and 2024. China, Romania, and versions of the Russian team also won women's team gold during that period.

ALWAYS EVOLVING

For a time, gymnastics team competitions in the Olympics involved athletes performing together as a group. Today, individual gymnasts perform routines, and the scores are added together to form a team total. There have been other notable changes to the sport over the years. Music was added to women's floor routines prior to the 1960 Olympics in Rome, Italy. The 2000 Games in Sydney, Australia, dropped compulsory routines. These were standard routines in which gymnasts demonstrated they could master certain skills.

Over the years, the number of gymnasts on each team has varied. Teams dropped from seven to six gymnasts at the 2000 Olympics. In 2012 and 2016, each team had five gymnasts. Then, for the Tokyo Olympics in 2021, countries could bring as many as six gymnasts. However, only four could take part in the

TRAMPOLINE GYMNASTICS

Trampoline became the third Olympic gymnastics discipline starting at the 2000 Games. Men's and women's gymnasts perform routines while bouncing on large trampolines. While airborne, athletes combine forward and backward flips with dizzying spins. China leads all countries with four Olympic gold medals and 16 total medals. Rosie MacLennan of Canada became the first trampoline gymnast to successfully defend an Olympic gold medal. She won in 2012 and again in 2016.

team competition. The sport returned to five-person teams for the 2024 Games.

Another change in Olympic gymnastics was implemented ahead of the 2008 Games. Throughout much of gymnastics history, routines were scored on a 10-point scale. But the new system is open-ended. This means there is officially no

Brazil's Rebeca Andrade twists onto the vault table during the women's vault final at the 2024 Olympics. She won silver in the event.

At the 2024 Games, Carlos Yulo made history by winning gold on floor and vault. He became the first male athlete from the Philippines to win a gold medal.

maximum score. Gymnasts are now judged based on the difficulty and execution of each routine. The loss of the perfect 10 score saddened many gymnastics fans. However, officials deemed the new scoring system to be fairer.

Yet the biggest change to gymnastics over the years has been the sport itself. Gymnasts are constantly pushing the limits of the sport. With every new year, the athletes are performing more challenging and innovative routines. Fans around the world continue to be mesmerized by gymnasts' athleticism, power, artistry, and strength.

CHAPTER 3

EARLY POWERS AND ICONS

There were no gyms where Alberto Braglia grew up in northern Italy. So at age 12, he began teaching himself gymnastics in his family's barn. The sport was a natural fit. By the 1908 Olympics in London, he was considered one of the best in the world.

Gymnasts had only two competitions at that time, an individual and a team event. That year's individual all-around competition included seven routines on five apparatuses. Showcasing amazing form and artistry, Braglia cruised to the gold medal. At the next Olympics four years later in Stockholm, Sweden, he was even better. This time he won gold in both the team and individual events. Judges scored him particularly well on the high bar.

Braglia was a gymnastics star. His life was much different than today's top gymnasts, though. In need of money between Olympics, Braglia began performing stunts as a character

After competing at the Olympics, Alberto Braglia helped coach the Italian men's gymnastics team to gold at the 1932 Games in Los Angeles.

called "The Bullet Man." Gymnastics officials briefly banned him from the sport. They said he violated rules at the time that said Olympians had to be amateurs. Later in life, Braglia became an acrobat and performed in the circus.

SOVIET DYNASTIES

Upon its founding in the early 1900s, the Soviet Union refused to take part in the Olympics. Its leaders viewed the Games as being biased toward Western nations, especially the United States. But after World War II, the Soviets viewed sports differently. They saw the Olympics as an opportunity to show their strength as a country. So at the 1952 Games in Helsinki, Finland, a Soviet team took part.

Much about the Soviet Union was a mystery to people outside the country. Reports from within the Soviet Union told of great athletic feats there. But few people had actually seen those feats. It only added to the intrigue when the Soviet Union and other Eastern Bloc teams stayed at a separate athletes' village in Helsinki. The Eastern Bloc was a group of countries closely aligned with the Soviet Union.

The Soviet athletes proved to be quite successful in Helsinki. Only the United States won more medals. The sporting rivalry between the two nations became a major theme in coming Olympics. As was the case in real life, each country wanted to

Viktor Chukarin of the Soviet Union medaled in four of the six apparatus finals at the 1952 Games.

show it was the true world power. When it came to gymnastics, though, there was no question which country was stronger.

Viktor Chukarin had been a soldier for the Soviet Union during World War II. After being captured and spending four years as a prisoner of war, he was released in 1945. Chukarin soon resumed training as a gymnast. By 1952, he was already 30 years old. Yet his gymnastics towered above that of his competition. Chukarin won six medals in Helsinki, including the team and all-around gold medals. He then defended both gold medals at the 1956 Olympics in Melbourne, Australia. His 11 total medals, including seven golds, helped establish the Soviet men as a gymnastics force.

Behind Mariya Gorokhovskaya, the Soviet women made a statement debut of their own at the 1952 Olympics. Gorokhovskaya earned the all-around title and finished second in all four apparatus finals at those Games. Her performance also boosted the Soviet women to the first of eight consecutive team gold medals. The women's program at the time also included a team portable apparatus event. It was similar to what is now rhythmic gymnastics. And Gorokhovskaya earned a gold medal in that event as well. She is still the only woman in any sport to win seven medals in a single Olympics.

Larisa Latynina carried on the Soviet dynasty after that. She thrived during an era when the sport was more balletic and less acrobatic. Making her Olympic debut at age 21, Latynina won the 1956 all-around title. It was one of six medals and four golds that she won in Melbourne. Her final Olympics came in 1964 in Tokyo. By the end of those Games, Latynina owned an amazing 18 medals. Half of them were gold, including another all-around

BACK-TO-BACK

Czechoslovakia's Věra Čáslavská entranced fans with her gymnastics. She also drew both praise and consequences for standing up for her beliefs. The Czech star won 11 medals during her three Olympics in 1960, 1964, and 1968. She is the last woman to win all-around gold in consecutive Games. However, Čáslavská faced ill treatment at home after speaking out against the Soviet Union's influence in Czechoslovakia.

Soviet gymnast Larisa Latynina won consecutive all-around golds in 1956 and 1960 and won all-around silver in 1964.

title from the 1960 Games. Her total medal count stood as the record among all sports for nearly 50 years. American swimmer Michael Phelps finally surpassed Latynina's total in 2012.

RISE OF JAPAN

The Soviet men's dominance had barely begun when a powerful new rival emerged. Japan claimed the team silver medal in 1956. Then the team secured gold at the next five consecutive Olympics. The Soviet Union finished as runner-up each time.

A few years into Japan's run, a junior high student named Sawao Kato tried the high bar during physical education class.

WILL TO WIN

At the 1976 Olympics, Shun Fujimoto landed awkwardly on floor exercise. In that instant, his kneecap shattered. Japan's hope for a fifth consecutive men's team gold medal appeared unlikely. However, Fujimoto battled through the pain. He scored well on pommel horse. Then he performed one of his best routines ever on the still rings. It ended with a hard landing from nearly 8 feet (2.4 m). Behind Fujimoto's performance, Japan went on to secure its fifth straight gold medal.

Afterward, his teacher suggested that Kato join the local gymnastics club. Before long, Kato was Japan's biggest star. He became known for his disciplined training methods. Kato worked hard to perfect his technique. But what most set him apart was his presence. Kato performed his gymnastics with a distinct sense of artistry. This style later came to define Japanese gymnasts.

In 1968, Kato made his Olympic debut at age 22 in Mexico City, Mexico. Over the course of three Olympics, he won 12 medals. Among them were back-to-back golds in the all-around in 1968 and 1972. And he nearly became the first man to win that title three times. However, Kato fell just short with a silver at the 1976 Games in Montreal, Canada. Still, his eight gold medals remain a record for men's gymnastics.

A WOMEN'S REVOLUTION

Soviet women dominated during the 1950s and 1960s. But their performances did not capture a lot of attention outside the

Eastern Bloc. The sport emphasized dancing elements more than high-flying acrobatics. The Soviet stars also came off as serious and distant. Olga Korbut changed all of that.

At 17, Korbut was younger than most gymnasts at the 1972 Games in Munich, West Germany. And her gymnastics was different. Korbut's routines were acrobatic and individualistic. She performed daring moves nobody else had ever tried. She also showed off her personality in a way few others did at that time. The combination captivated fans. Korbut won three gold medals and a silver in Munich. But it was her personality, flair, and acrobatic skills that made her a superstar.

Korbut returned for the 1976 Olympics. Once again, her skills and charm captivated fans. However, a teen from Romania stole the show. At 14 years old, Nadia Comăneci built on Korbut's exciting new style. She also upped the scoring. During the team competition, Comăneci zipped around the uneven bars with precision. The judges couldn't find anything wrong with her routine. They awarded Comăneci the first perfect 10 in Olympic gymnastics history.

Comăneci combined amazing technical skills with creativity. Over the course of those Games, she scored seven perfect 10s. She also won five medals, including golds in the all-around, uneven bars, and balance beam finals. Suddenly, people around the world couldn't seem to get enough gymnastics.

Romania's Nadia Comăneci was inducted into the International Gymnastics Hall of Fame in 1993.

The early 1980s were a difficult time for the Olympics. Comăneci added four more medals at the 1980 Games. But those Olympics were overshadowed by politics. In 1979, the Soviet Union invaded Afghanistan. In protest, the United States and several other countries boycotted the 1980 Olympics. Four years later, Los Angeles hosted the next Summer Games. In response, the Soviets led a boycott of those Olympics.

The boycott meant some of the sport's top stars stayed home. However, it also created an opportunity for the United States. In front of enthusiastic home crowds, the Americans took advantage. They led all countries in gymnastics with 16 medals. That included the first team gold medal for the

US men's team. But no athlete saw their star power shine more at the 1984 Games than Mary Lou Retton. An American woman had never won an Olympic medal in gymnastics. In Los Angeles, Retton won five. Fans were drawn to the spirited teen and her fast and powerful style.

Retton's most dramatic performance came in the all-around final. Romania's Ecaterina Szabo held a 9.95-point lead with only Retton to go. The American would need to be near-perfect on her vault to tie Szabo. And her full-twisting Tsukahara was perfect. Retton stuck the landing. With a score of 10, Retton just barely clinched the all-around gold medal. And with that, she became one of the United States' most iconic Olympians.

Mary Lou Retton became known as "America's Sweetheart" after her success at the 1984 Olympics.

CHAPTER 4

ONWARD AND UPWARD

By the mid-1990s, the US women's team was loaded with talent. In 1994, Dominique Dawes became the first woman to win all five titles at the US championships. Attention turned to Dominique Moceanu the following year. At 13 years old, she became the youngest US all-around champion. Then there was Shannon Miller. As a shy 15-year-old, she had won five medals, including all-around silver, at the 1992 Olympics. Miller got even better after that. Between 1993 and 1994, she won five world titles. That included the all-around championship each year.

All this talent was coming together at the perfect time. The 1996 Olympics were on home soil in Atlanta. Winning the country's first women's team gold medal would not be easy, though. China, Romania, and Russia all brought strong squads.

Fans packed into the Georgia Dome to cheer on the home team. The Americans, later named the "Magnificent Seven,"

Team USA's Shannon Miller ended her Olympic career with seven medals, including two golds.

boasted depth and experience. Three gymnasts were back from the 1992 Olympic team. And five of the seven members were 18 or older. Their abilities showed throughout the team event. With just two routines to go, the Americans had victory in their sights. But then, disaster struck.

Moceanu, a fan favorite throughout the Games, fell on both her vaults. Only Kerri Strug remained. At 18, Strug was competing in her second Olympics. Compared to some of her teammates, though, she was not talked about as much. That was usually just fine for the reserved teen. But suddenly, all eyes were squarely on her.

The Magnificent Seven were inducted into the USA Gymnastics Hall of Fame in 1998.

Gathering her composure, Strug raced down the runway, pushed off the vault, and fell. Even worse, the fall had strained her left ankle. And with the Russians still competing, it looked like they had a chance to win. A higher score from Strug could ensure the gold medal.

So with 32,048 fans looking on, Strug gathered herself once again. She raced down the runway for her second vault. This time, she stuck it. After saluting the judges, Strug crumbled to the mat in pain. The vault upped Team USA's score. It turned out the Americans would have won without it. But Strug's grit and selflessness endeared her to fans. The Magnificent Seven made history as the first US women's team to claim the gold medal. Strug, meanwhile, became a US Olympic icon.

UPS AND DOWNS DOWN UNDER

During the women's all-around final at the 2000 Olympics in Sydney, gymnasts kept falling on vault. Among them was Svetlana Khorkina. The Russian superstar had come into the Games as the favorite for gold. Instead, the fall rattled Khorkina. Later, the usually ultra-confident gymnast fell again on the uneven bars, her signature event.

Eventually, officials figured out the problem. The vault had been set too low. Affected gymnasts were given the opportunity to redo that rotation. But it was too late for Khorkina. Too shaken to try again, she declined and settled for 10th.

Khorkina retired as the world's most decorated female gymnast. One of the few major titles she never won was Olympic all-around gold. However, she did get some redemption. The 2000 event finals took place in the days after the all-around. Khorkina had won gold on the uneven bars in 1996. In Sydney, she was back to her best. A taller gymnast, Khorkina's inventive skills set her apart as she successfully defended her title.

SUPER SCHERBO

Vitaly Scherbo was nearly perfect at the 1992 Olympics. The Belarus-born gymnast first led the Unified Team, made up of athletes from the former Soviet Union, to men's team gold. Then he won all-around gold. A few days after that, he won the pommel horse, rings, vault, and parallel bars all on the same night. Scherbo's six gold medals in a single Olympics remains a record for gymnastics. And four years later, he won four more medals, all of which were bronze.

SETTING THE STANDARD

Success has come in spurts for the US men's team. In 1984, Bart Conner and Peter Vidmar won gold medals on the parallel bars and pommel horse, respectively. The Americans also claimed team gold that year. Eight years later, in 1992, Trent Dimas joined the gold-medal club on high bar. It took 12 more years for another gymnast to join that golden group.

Paul Hamm arrived at his second Olympics in 2004 as the defending world all-around champion. But any hopes of repeating as champion looked shot in the fourth rotation of the all-around final. A fall on vault dropped him to 12th place. Hamm never gave up, though. Masterful routines on the parallel bars and high bar propelled him back to first place. That made him the first US man to win all-around gold.

It was a bittersweet celebration, however. Controversy broke out when it was determined that another gymnast had

In addition to his all-around gold, Paul Hamm won silver on high bar and silver in the team final at the 2004 Games.

been underscored. Many people pressured Hamm to give up his gold medal. After a formal review, the original result stood. Hamm remained the Olympic champion.

HOME, SWEET HOME

China long had a conflicting relationship with the Games. For many years, the country did not send athletes to compete. But by the 2000s, the Chinese saw the Olympics as an opportunity. The world's most populated country was an emerging power. Hosting a successful Olympics could demonstrate that. So could an excellent performance by its athletes. In 2008, China got that opportunity when the Games came to Beijing.

China's men had never won Olympic team gold. But on home soil, they dominated. The team's star Yang Wei led China to victory over Japan in the team final. The Chinese men also won six of the seven individual gold medals.

The women's competition proved to be just as thrilling. The United States had two superstars in Nastia Liukin and Shawn Johnson. They would go on to win gold and silver in the all-around, respectively. But China was strong, too. Competing in the same rotation, the teams went toe to toe. Both had a fall on balance beam. But going into the final rotation on floor, gold remained up for grabs. A few mistakes by the US gymnasts gave China an opening. China's star Cheng Fei led

From 2009 to 2015, Kohei Uchimura of Japan won six straight all-around gold medals at the World Championships.

them through. The home fans rejoiced as the Chinese women became Olympic champions. And by the end of the Games, they would add another gold plus four bronze medals.

KING KOHEI

Kohei Uchimura of Japan won the men's all-around silver medal at the 2008 Games. Shortly after, he became nearly unstoppable. "King Kohei" competed in four Olympics, winning seven medals. Many consider him to be the best male gymnast of all time.

What set Uchimura apart was his technical mastery. He made the most difficult skills in the world look elegant and easy. He also came through when it mattered most. All that showed at the 2016 Olympics. First, he led Japan to team gold. Next up was the all-around final. A win would make Uchimura the first man to claim back-to-back golds in the event since Sawao Kato in 1968 and 1972. Through five rotations, Uchimura trailed Ukraine's Oleg Verniaiev. Then, it all came down to high bar. And in a dramatic and daring performance, Uchimura nailed the day's most difficult high bar routine to clinch the gold medal.

At the 2012 Games, Gabby Douglas became the first American gymnast to win gold in both the all-around and team finals.

BEST IN CLASS

In 2012, the US women arrived in London on a mission. By then, Americans routinely competed for gold medals in individual events. But after the Magnificent Seven in 1996, US teams kept falling just short of victory. At the 2012 Olympics, however, the "Fierce Five" made sure that changed.

The Americans set the tone in the first rotation. The Amanar vault involves 2.5 twists. It is so difficult that only a few women even attempted it. Yet in London, all three Americans nailed the vault. McKayla Maroney's Amanar was so high and well executed that fans in the arena gasped. The US coach at that time called it the best vault ever.

No one came close to catching the Americans after that. With each rotation, they added to their lead. Jordyn Weiber, Gabby Douglas, and Aly Raisman's closing floor routines were essentially a victory lap. Along with Maroney and Kyla Ross, the Fierce Five combined for one of the most dominant team performances in Olympic history.

Douglas and Raisman were still among the best in the world in 2016. Meanwhile, Simone Biles had won the previous three world titles. Those three gymnasts, along with Laurie Hernandez and Madison Kocian, showed up at the Rio Games as the overwhelming favorites. And once again, the US team delivered. The Americans rolled through their 12 routines

POMMEL HORSE HERO

Stephen Nedoroscik went to the 2024 Games with one job. He was on Team USA to compete only on pommel horse. And in the men's team final, pommel horse was the last rotation for the Americans. That meant Nedoroscik had to wait. Cameras showed him sitting with his eyes closed. Finally, he stood up, removed his glasses, and hit his very difficult routine to clinch the bronze medal for the United States. It was the US men's first gymnastics team medal in 16 years. A few days later, Nedoroscik won an individual bronze on pommel horse.

without a major mistake. Biles, who went on to win three individual gold medals plus a bronze, contributed four of those routines. And as in London, nobody came close to catching the Americans.

Most people expected a three-peat from Team USA. However, the postponed Tokyo Olympics in 2021 brought unique challenges. For the US team, that included Biles suffering from "the twisties." After she withdrew from the team final, the Americans regrouped to win silver. Then at the 2024 Games, Olympians Biles, Suni Lee, Jordan Chiles, and Jade Carey were back, along with newcomer Hezly Rivera. The crowds were back, too. With fans cheering in the stands in Paris, the US team proved once again that it was the best in the world.

The Americans started the night off on vault. They set the tone with a dominant showing on the event. The US women continued to shine throughout the team final. Even with a fall

The US women pose with their gold medals after winning the team final at the 2024 Olympics.

on beam for Chiles, the United States held a commanding lead going into the fourth rotation. Fittingly, it all came down to Biles on floor. Thundering through her tumbling passes, Biles put Tokyo behind her with a thrilling, high-flying performance. When it was over, she paused on the floor to smile and blow kisses to the fans. Moments later, her score flashed on the screen. The US women's team celebrated as Olympic champions once again.

GLOSSARY

acrobatic
Difficult body movements, such as balancing, jumping, and tumbling.

amateur
A person who plays a sport without getting paid.

apparatus
A piece of equipment used in gymnastics.

artistry
An artistic quality, skill, or performance.

boycott
To refuse to take part in an event as a form of protest.

debut
First appearance.

dynasty
A team that has an extended period of success, usually winning multiple championships in the process.

iconic
Well-known for excellence.

modern
Recent times.

pandemic
A widespread outbreak of a disease that affects a large portion of the population.

rivalry
A fierce and ongoing competition between two opponents.

routine
A set performance by a gymnast on one apparatus.

stuck
When a gymnast ends the routine by landing without needing to hop or take a step.

tumbling
Moving gymnastics elements such as flips and handsprings.

MORE INFORMATION

BOOKS

Lawrence, Blythe. *The History of Gymnastics*. Abdo, 2021.

Price, Karen. *GOATs of Olympic Sports*. Abdo, 2022.

Stevenson, Robin. *Kid Olympians, Summer*. Quirk, 2024.

ONLINE RESOURCES

Booklinks
NONFICTION NETWORK
FREE! ONLINE NONFICTION RESOURCES

To learn more about Olympic gymnastics, please visit **abdobooklinks.com** or scan this QR code. These links are routinely monitored and updated to provide the most current information available.

INDEX

ABOUT THE AUTHOR

Chrös McDougall is a sportswriter, author, and book editor who focuses on Olympic and Paralympic sports. A gymnastics dropout, he went on to cover the sport at the University of Missouri and then at the elite level, including at the 2008 and 2021 Olympic Games. He lives in Minneapolis, Minnesota, with his wife, two children, and a boxer named Eira who is always a Perfect 10.